LET YOUR SOUL SHINE

Reflections on Love & Happiness

NANCY MARLOWE

DEDICATION

In honor of Liam and those who love deeply.

ABOUT NANCY MARLOWE

Nancy Marlowe is a Psychic Medium of verified accuracy who uses remote viewing, mental telepathy and clairvoyance to locate everything from missing people to hidden treasure. A native of East Texas, she applies her special talent for psychic profiling to salvage relationships and to help foster new ones.

Saved from death by an Angel, Nancy felt compelled to become a professional Psychic Medium. Using her experience as a "teacher of teachers" and Charter School educator, Nancy uses her teaching experience to help people understand the Afterlife.

Nancy is a magna cum laude graduate and a member of Phi Beta Kappa. An accomplished speaker, she is available to speak at conferences and workshops in your area.

Table of Contents

WHAT PEOPLE ARE SAYING

"I am a true believer that everything happens for a reason—understanding and accepting those reasons are what prove difficult. Being deeply spiritual, and intuitive myself—Nancy provides me with the affirmation that what I am experiencing is natural to my being.

When I feel my world closing in on me, Nancy is there to show me the light and my own undeniable force. She has proven to be the spiritual guide that I need to help me become the person that I am destined to be."

Victoria Williams, San Diego, California

"Nancy was wonderful. She knew a lot of things that there is no way she could have found out that information elsewhere. She is very sweet and caring.

I now feel more in touch with the Other Side than ever."

Emily Reyes, Phoenix, Arizona

"I feel fortunate to have located Nancy Marlowe. The reading was very emotional and intense for me."

Craig Saunders, Honolulu, Hawaii

"I visited Nancy three times with my sister, husband, and friend and each time I was truly amazed! We laughed, cried, and left with a sense of closure and closeness. My husband is no longer a skeptic."

Anna Lancaster, Madison, Wisconsin

"Nancy Marlowe has read for me for over ten years. She is astonishingly accurate each and every time. She is amazing and honest. I cannot recommend her and her skills highly enough!"

Karen Collins, Washington, D.C.

"Thank you so much. I don't know what I would have done without you.

You were the lifeline I needed."

Laura Daniels, Boston, Massachusetts

"Nancy is an amazing reader. She gave very descriptive details of my two boys who are both unique individuals.

I highly recommend her because of her accuracy and compassion."

Kim Anderson, Houston, Texas

"Mike has enrolled in some college real estate courses and already has internships with two different real estate companies. He has listened to the tape of his reading with you several times and feels that your input has made a big contribution to solidifying his direction.

And, also I wanted to thank you for my own recent personal reading. It was very meaningful reassurance and particularly hit home when you suggested that I relax and enjoy instead of being guarded and trying to find things that are not going well in the relationship.

You make a difference in people's lives ... we are two of those people!"

Michelle Lorraine, Newport Beach, California

"Thank you so much for the beautiful reading you gave my friend Sara. She was so thankful to meet you the same way I was. In addition to the wonderful reading, she found spending time with you to be so peaceful, calming and warm. You truly are a gifted soul. We thank God for sending such an angel to this earth and for allowing our paths to cross."

Renee Williams, San Diego, California

INTRODUCTION

"We are constantly in transition … traveling toward unconditional love. This is our purpose."

Dear Fellow Traveler,

Welcome to Earth School. Here you will learn through experience and observation.

Some of your lessons will be easy, fun and joyful. Some lessons will be hard, very hard. We learn from both kinds of lessons.

As in any quality education, the lessons you learn will not only expand your knowledge, but leave you with a thirst to know even more about your soul, your creator, and your reason for being.

During your years on Earth spent living as a human, you will become aware of "a little voice" inside your head. This voice is not your imagination. The voice you hear whispering to you is real.

Get Quiet. Be still. Close your eyes. Listen to the voice inside. This voice will guide you and give you peace throughout your journey on Earth.

"Let Your Soul Shine" contains a collection of inspirational poems and stories. Some of the stories are yours. Some are mine.

It's a book about us.

It is my fondest hope that you will truly understand how wonderful you are and how much you matter … to everything that is. The very fact that you exist on this Earth is a miracle.

Thank you for being in my life.

I love you.

Nancy Marlowe

LET YOUR SOUL SHINE

1

WHO AM I REALLY?

"You already are who you want to be."

Have you ever wondered who you are?

I have. I suppose that is because most of my life, I didn't know who I really was.

You see, when I was a child, I didn't know I was different because I could see dead people. Matter of fact, I thought everybody else was seeing dead people too.

Imagine how it was. Day after day, I saw shadows dart across the room and orbs floating through the air. I knew what people were thinking and what they intended to do. There was nothing unusual about any of this to me.

But then one day things changed. I realized I was different.

I was about nine years old when it occurred to me that other people in my life weren't seeing the orbs and shadows too. They didn't feel unseen people press against their body like I did. They didn't hear voices when there was seemingly nobody there.

So I did what any kid nine-year old would do to play it safe. I shut everything out. It was like turning off a light switch.

The voices I heard went silent. The shadows slowed down and only every now and then would an orb drift by. The curtain had fallen on the stage of my invisible world. It did not go up again until I was in my late forties. That's when I finally understood who I really was.

Picture it. I grew up in the Bible Belt where religion was a huge portion of people's lives. Saving your soul was a big thing in those parts. Going to Heaven and doing what you had to do to save your eternal soul was preached far and wide. I attended church, studied the Bible, and was baptized. It's what most people did where I lived. It was expected.

After all, if you weren't saved, everybody knew your soul would go straight to Hell. This was my introduction to the human soul. It had to be saved or else.

I learned early on we were born sinners. God was wrathful, and you were doomed to burn in Hell for all Eternity if you didn't do exactly what the church said was necessary for salvation.

And get this. I went around feeling sorry for all the little children in other countries who didn't know the rules of soul saving. I worried their souls were doomed.

Poor little kids. They weren't going to be allowed in Heaven like I was. That's right. All those poor little innocent children were going to Hell. Their souls were automatically damned forever just because they didn't know the church rules. Every time I saw a new "National Geographic" magazine with pictures of other children from other countries, I would worry about all those little children. In fact, I worried a lot. Scary to think about, isn't it? Sad, too.

Years have passed now. Thankfully things have changed. Now I am grown. My children are grown, and I have a grandson.

Oh, something else has changed too. A good thing.

I'm talking to dead people again. In fact, I am a professional psychic medium. I don't worry about saving my soul anymore.

Today I just want to be the soul that I am. I want to rejoice in who I am as a person. I want to feel free and happy. And like all of us, I want to know I am loved.

Over the years, I've done thousands of readings for people all over the world. Many of them come to me feeling lost, not knowing who they are. They feel alone and scared and don't know what to do with their lives.

They say, "I feel like I don't belong. I feel like I am from somewhere else." They ask with pleading eyes, "Can you tell me where I come from? Can you tell me who I really am?"

So the next writing is for those of you who have ever felt lost and wondered who you really are.

Welcome home.

I AM YOUR SOUL

"You are wiser than the wisest sage who ever lived.
You are the voice of truth.
And you are here to become even wiser."

How do we know something exists? We can see the skin on our arms, and the curl of our eyelashes. We can even see our breath on a cold winter's day. But we cannot see our soul.

However, since the dawn of time, man has acknowledged the existence of the soul. We mention the soul in songs, religion, poems, media, and philosophy. You have probably heard phrases like soul man, touch your soul, lost soul, poor soul, free soul, saved soul, rock your soul.

Poems of great poets touch our souls. Priests will tell you the soul can be saved. A flower child of the sixties will proclaim that the soul is meant to be free. Yet the soul remains elusive, a far-off thing that doesn't seem to be a part of us. But, the soul is a part of us.

We know it is there and have always known it was there. We sense it. We can feel it. We understand what all the soul phrases mean. We intuitively know we have a soul … somewhere.

However, although we know we have a soul, we don't think about the soul very much. It is just something we are supposed to have. But have you ever wondered where the soul is and what it does all day? Have you ever asked yourself what is a soul? I have.

One day, I became very curious. I really wanted to discover more about this thing called a soul.

So one beautiful morning while meditating, I decided to ask the Universe about the soul. Where is the soul located? What was its purpose?

With great reverence and a whole lot of awe, I gathered up all my courage and asked, "What is a soul? Where does it hang out? Is it a part of me?"

I even said out loud, "Hey Soul, I really want to get to know you. If you are there, talk to me."

What happened next seemed impossible. To my astonishment my Soul replied!

You wanted to talk to me.
I am here.
I am your soul.

I am not some far off distant thing like you think I am.
And am I not a figment of your imagination either.
I'm very real.

You hear me talking to you every day.

I am the little voice inside your head.
You ignore me most of the time.
But that voice in your head is me,
The voice of your soul.

I am always with you.
You don't have to ask to talk to me.
I'll talk to you even if you don't ask.

Who am I?

I am you.
The real you.
The invisible part of you.

I have many homes.
At this moment, my home is in your body.
This is why your head echoes with the sound of my voice.

I know being human is very hard sometimes.
It's also wonderful.
Even magical.

I understand you.
And I love you just the way you are.
It is my job to look out for you.
To guide you.

Heaven wants you to know how much you are needed.

You are the stuff that stars are made of.
You are the spores of a dandelion.
You are the wheat ripening in a field.

You matter.

It is time for you to see your beauty.
Time for you to awaken to your birthright.
It's time to be you.

My precious one, you are greatly needed.
Your world is on the brink of destruction
With wars, greed, and weapons of mass destruction.

Some of your greatest beasts,
The polar bears, rhinos, and snow leopards
Are nearly extinct.

Your rain forests are shrinking.
They are being pillaged and burned for profit.
Humans frack the earth in search of oil and gas
Causing earthquakes.
Global warming has altered the climate of the world.

The earth we gave you
Is no longer--
The earth we gave you.

Heaven needs your help.
Your neighbor needs your help.
Your planet needs your help.

We are truly in this together.
And together
We must rise.

I'm glad you wanted to talk to me today.
I would like to talk with you more often.
You see, we need each other, you and me.

Let me explain more about our special relationship.
Right now, you are living in a human body.
But your body is not you.

The body you occupy has a remarkable brain.
It acts as a computer
Calculating, storing, and analyzing information.
But your brain is not you.

The brain has different levels of operation:
The conscious
And the subconscious mind.

The mind is a product of the brain's activity.
It is the part of the brain that thinks.
But your mind is not you either.

Your human personality is ego driven.
It is fed by human emotion
And human experience.

The ego likes to tell you who you are
And who you are not.
The ego likes to dominate.

To maintain control,
The ego instills fear.
It tells you what and how
To think about the world.

The ego makes you doubt yourself.
It destroys your confidence.
But your ego is not you--
No matter what your ego says.

So who are you really?
You are a soul living inside a human body
On planet Earth.

You are the life force for the body you now occupy.
One day you will leave your body
And rejoin your creator.

Like your creator
You are made of pure light energy.
And since you are made of light,
You are a Light Being.

Light Beings are powerful.
Very powerful.
Remember to use your power wisely.

Together,
You and your creator
Can do remarkable things.

Just like your creator,
You, too, have the power to create.
Your thoughts, ideas, intentions, and desires create.

You must use your power to create a better world.

This is why you continually ask,
"What is my purpose?"
You intuitively know
You are here to create a better world.

The most important thing for you to remember is this:
Like your creator
You are limitless love.

Be the love that you are on Earth.

Your love will give others hope.
Peace.
Joy.
Inspiration
When they need it most.

To fulfill your purpose
Just be you.
A being of light.
A soul.

You matter to everything that is
And will ever be.
You are.

And just like that, my meditation was over. I opened my eyes and began to notice the familiar things around me. The minute hand on the wall clock still ticked. The distant whisper of traffic could still be heard outside my window. The red geraniums in their terracotta pot looked just as happy as they had before.

Yet something life altering had happened.

My soul spoke to me today-- and this time, I heard.

3

JUST THE WAY YOU ARE

"I am accepted just the way I am. Imagine that."

When my children were little, they loved to watch the TV show, "Mr. Roger's Neighborhood." Do you remember it? Mr. Rogers always smiled and spoke in a soft pleasant voice. He always had interesting things to say. With genuine kindness and comforting warmth, he taught children the value of friendship, community, and love.

Everything Mr. Rogers said was spoken in a simple, matter-of-fact way. It was as if he were stating the simple truths about living a good life and being a good neighbor. He taught children that they mattered, as did all the rest of the people in the world.

"I like you just the way you are," Mr. Rogers said to his young audience every day. So as the days and years rolled by, and the children grew, every day they heard him say, "I like you just the way you are."

Mr. Rogers was a wise man. He must have been a very Old Soul.

He didn't say, "I like you but..." or "I will like you when..." or "I will like you if..." "He didn't say any of those things at all. Instead, Mr. Rogers put a warm smile on his face, looked straight into the camera's eye, and said sincerely to his audience, "I like you just the way you are."

What an important message to deliver to the children of the world (and to the parents of the children who watched the show with them).

Mr. Rogers let his audience know they were accepted and loved with that one powerful sentence, "I like you just the way you are."

Mr. Rogers left an important imprint on the world. He taught us about unconditional love. He taught us we mattered.

What a wonderful legacy to leave behind for the people of the world: "You matter."

I miss Mr. Rogers.

NO MATTER WHAT

*"Don't you think it's wonderful
that we get to keep trying until we get it right?"*

*Have no fear.
You will find a way.
You are not alone.
Things will get better … and better … and better.*

*Meanwhile,
You can make a difference to somebody else.
You can do more than you think you can do.*

*Remember
You were created by God.*

You are made of light.
God light.

You are a Soul.
A part of Higher Consciousness.
A messenger of love.

Just like God
You are the skies.
The mountains.
All that is.

Take comfort.
Be at peace.
Exhibit grace.

You are the light
Of God
Shining on Earth.

No matter where you go.
No matter what you do.
No matter how broken you think you are.
You exist because you were wanted by God.

You will be loved.
Always.
No matter what.

5

TIME TO BE ME

"Filled with quiet contentment and peace, I am."

Do you make time for yourself?

Or are you like I used to be, working, driving, and rushing around with little or no *me time*?

How difficult is it for you to slow down and listen to what your heart is telling you?

If you already make *me time* a priority in your life, please accept my warmest congratulations. You are connected to the source of all life. You are connected to your soul. Your spirit and your life are most likely flourishing. What a victory that the digital age hasn't gobbled you up yet.

Most of us have to turn our technological devices off at some point and break free of the "electronic leash" with its demanding beeping and ringing. We need quiet time where we can sit alone in lovely silence and just be.

I guess that's why we call our little retreats a getaway. We all have to do it from time to time. We have to get away from the busy lives we lead. Our happiness and wellbeing depend on tranquility and quiet reflection.

But technology is so captivating it's hard to pry me away from my computer. In fact, I use the computer so much, I often wonder if I'm addicted to the thing.

And cell phones? They are another technological marvel that has taken over our lives. But what would we do without them? Can you imagine your life without your cell phone? I can't. Cell phones and computers have connected us to the rest of the world in ways we would have never thought possible.

Other aspects of technology have become a part of our daily lives, even seemingly "old" ones like television, radio, fax machines, and scanners. Now we depend on electronic signature apps, digital hearing aids, iCloud, Skype, and Kindle.

Then there is social media. What would we do without that? Oh, dear, we simply have to have social media, too.

You see, I absolutely love my computer and my cell phone. I love listening to music on Pandora or watching funny videos on YouTube. I really enjoy all the information that is available to me at the touch of a computer button. My gosh, just look at Kindle. Look at Google!

I must say it is wonderful having this kind of technology in my life. It is a good, good thing.

But sometimes I feel bombarded by too much information. I feel bad knowing my privacy has been invaded by government and corporate surveillance which track, monitor, record, and spy on my every Google search, phone call, email, Facebook post, you name it. Remember when a cookie was a delicious baked good? Now the non-edible variety is dropped into a folder inside your computer every time you visit a website. That's how corporations know what kind of ads to put on your Facebook sidebar.

Yes, it feels like technology is always watching, always monitoring, always gathering and collating information about me. Little ole me.

Here's the thing though. Speaking personally, technology has greatly improved my way of life. However, I am on my computer so many hours a day, I don't always take time for myself. I have to force myself to push away from the computer and go exercise, or meditate, or call a friend.

That's right. I get so caught up on the computer, I sometimes forget to take time out for me. Then my soul suffers anguish because I have lost touch with it. I have forgotten about me. Who I am. What I want. What is important in life.

Then I find myself a little depressed. I fail to thrive, and discover that I've become isolated. I wake up in the morning feeling miserable until one day I find myself thinking, "What happened to Nancy? Where did she go? Why is she so sad? Oh my! Did the computer gobble her up?"

Yes, technology is a great thing. But … I have a habit of overdoing. That's when I have to remember to take time out for myself, to be myself, to think, to breathe, to play, to meditate, to go for long walks, to get away from it all.

And that's what I do. I turn everything off. I sit with stillness and surrender to the silence.

There aren't enough words to describe how much I relish this peaceful time. It is in stillness that I become whole again. In my temple of self-imposed solitude, I am strengthened by prayer, reflection, and meditation.

In stillness, I remember who I am and where I come from. Stillness restores my soul.

You see, by slowing down the pace of my life, I find time to notice all for which I'm grateful. I feel renewed appreciation for my loved ones. With new eyes, I behold the pink blush of dawn. I relish the hot sweetened tea in my cup. I breathe in the spicy perfume of a candle that flickers on my desk. Even the music playing softly in the background is sweeter than it was before. My life feels sweeter, too. I feel alive and nourished, whole, and at peace.

One of the great things about being a medium is doing readings for people. Before each reading, I always meditate and connect with Heaven. This discipline of meditation pulls me away from my analytical, technology-loving mind, and sends me back "home" again.

When I meditate, I am able to connect with All That Is and All That Is Good. I go into a trance-like state where I feel as though I have one foot on Earth and the other foot in Heaven. It is sheer bliss to be in both dimensions at the same time.

Over the years, as I've come to understand more about what is truly important, I've learned that meditation is nourishment for the soul. It is truly an elixir for health and wellbeing.

In the peace and calm of meditation, I connect with Heaven and the loving energy of the Universe. Afterwards, I go for a walk by the ocean with my puppy. Content and at peace, my soul soars among the clouds and dances on sunlit waves. Lost in sublime tranquility, I find myself one with eternity.

Once again, all is well in Heaven and on Earth ... simply because I took time to be me.

6

GOT TO GET AWAY

"Time cannot be replaced. It cannot be bought
or sold. Time defines your existence."

Remember when life was easy
And there was time to laugh and play?
Yeah. I smiled a lot then.
I was happy all day.

There is so much noise now.
I can't even think.
So much going on
My spirits just sink.

There is no time to relax.
No time to wonder.

No pause for reflection
With all the stress I'm under.

Oh yeah, I've got a feeling
Deep inside of me.
This isn't the way
Life is supposed to be.

I remember the sunrise.
The dew on the lawn.
The peace and the joy
Of first light at dawn.

I want time to remember.
To follow my heart.
To live life with passion.
To get a new start.

I'm gonna turn off my cell phone
And unplug that TV.
I'm gonna log off the computer
And reconnect with me.

Oh yeah, I'm ready to set things right.
I'm ready to be free.
So I'm gonna take some time
To just be me.

Bye bye y'all.
See you later.
I'm gone.

7

ANGELS

"I am alive today because I cried out in the middle of the night, "God, help me!" and you know what? I was heard."

Do you believe in Angels?

Have you ever seen an Angel? Have you ever felt one around you? Have you read books about Angels? Used Angel cards? Do you have an Angel on top of your Christmas tree? If so, you are not alone. People all over the world believe in Angels.

Angels are a feel good thing.

In fact, just the thought of Angels makes me plain old happy. And if you get right down to it, I think most people feel the same way. After all, it's wonderful to know you are loved and protected and never alone. Thinking about Angels makes us feel good.

Seventy percent of Americans believe Angels are real. Yet to the other thirty percent of Americans, Angels are just a fantasy like Santa Claus or the Easter Bunny. You see, we really want to believe in Angels, but to some people, Angels just seem too good to be true.

So let me tell you a story. It is one of the most important stories of my life.

One day a Brinks armored vehicle slammed into my car.

The truck came out of nowhere and rear ended me so hard, my head snapped forward from the force. My seatbelt stopped me from smashing through the windshield, but my chest was filled with excruciating pain. I blacked out and went into shock.

An ambulance rushed me to the nearest hospital where I was X-rayed and released. I was told to go home because there was "nothing wrong with me."

Beaten up and bruised all over, I went home. Two weeks later, I woke up in the middle of the night, writhing in agony. The pain was brutal, constant, and piercing. I knew then that I was very seriously hurt.

I needed immediate help. Strange, isn't it, how without any experts telling us we're in danger, we know we are in a life threatening situation? The pain was so intense, I began to panic. Fear set in.

I didn't know where to turn or what to do and I sure didn't trust the local hospital that had released me so casually. I was a single woman with no family and few friends. Now I was alone in the middle of the night, badly hurt and in trouble.

Let's face it. Where do you turn when you know you could die without immediate help? Scared and helpless, I cried out in the dark, "Please help me. Help me! I need you!" With that cry for help, I added, "Please tell me the name of a doctor who can help me. I need this name by 8am so that I can call early for an appointment."

I understand now what an impossible request I had made. After all, I lived in Houston, Texas, which is a city of 6.6 million people. Prominent, respected doctors had waiting lists for months. But I had no time to lose. My life depended on being seen immediately, and I knew it.

At 8am, I called three different people. I asked each one if he or she knew of a good neurosurgeon. Each person gave me several names to choose from. To my surprise, on each person's list of referrals, the same name appeared. All three people gave me the name of Dr. David Baskin. But along with the recommendation, each person added, "You'll never get in to see him. People fly from all over the world to see him. He has a waiting list ten miles long."

I was desperate. I had nothing to lose. So I called his office and explained the wreck and the unbearable, terrifying pain I was in. Then I held my breath and asked, "Please. Would it be possible to see Dr. Baskin right away?"

Without hesitation, the office manager told me, "Yes. Go get an MRI, and I will arrange for Dr. Baskin to look at your pictures right away."

I made an appointment to get the MRI done immediately. The receptionist called me soon after the test was done and said, "Dr. Baskin has reviewed your MRI and wants to see you at once."

As I sat across the desk from him, I noticed that the doctor had a glow about him. Here was a man who had seen it all and felt it all. Yet instead of becoming cynical and hardened, Dr. Baskin was full of compassion, empathy, and hope.

I looked into his kind eyes and knew a Greater Power had sent me to the right person. I knew I was safe and protected.

Dr. Baskin explained that I needed to call in my family before he explained the injury because it was very serious.

In hushed tones, I told him there was nobody to call. I was alone, and I would get through this alone.

Dr. Baskin was silent for a moment. We sat there and stared at one another. Then he sighed.

"Here is what you are up against." He put the image of my cervical spine up on a lighted wall. "This is you," he said. "This is your skull, and this is your neck. Look at this section of your cervical spine. The C-5 disc is pressing on your spinal cord. You need surgery, and you need it right away. I won't sugarcoat this. It's very serious surgery."

Looking at the skeleton on the wall was a surreal experience. It was hard to believe that I was looking at me. It seemed as though I were looking at some anonymous body in a science book. This skeleton on the wall just couldn't be me.

But there it was. I could see a large disc pressing on the spinal cord. My spinal cord. Believe me, it was a frightening sight to behold.

Fear crept over me. The room spun. This awful thing was happening, and it was real. I looked at the MRI image again.

Suddenly a feeling of utter peace came over me as I sensed the presence of a strong, protective, male energy standing next to me. I could not see his face. But I could see the outline of his body. Towering above me, his presence felt majestic, and all-encompassing. His unearthly presence radiated a loving energy which filled the room with peace.

As if by magic, the invisible man communicated with me through a form of telepathy. Although no words came from his mouth, I could clearly hear his deep, reassuring voice. It was the most calm, comforting voice I have ever heard—almost like God was right there with me, standing by my side.

Although his kingly presence felt divine and powerful, I knew the invisible entity wasn't God. Stunned, I realized the presence standing next to me was an Angel.

Everything began to make sense. My prayer in the middle of the night had been answered by Heaven. I had been sent to this specific doctor by the Angel standing next to me.

It was then that I knew I would not go through the serious operation alone. My racing heart slowed down to a normal beat. My shoulders relaxed from around my head and all anxiety melted away. Fear was gone and tranquil peace took its place.

No matter how bleak the diagnosis was, I knew the final outcome. I would be restored to total health. The Angel standing next to me said so.

Miracle in the Operating Room

When Dr. Baskin cut into my neck during surgery at Methodist Hospital, he was stunned by what he saw. The C-5 cervical disc was not just pressing against the spinal cord, it was jammed up against it. What he discovered was "more than serious." It was lethal. How was I even alive?

The microscopic surgery to remove the disc took more than five hours. My cervical column was "fused" with the bone of a cadaver. Then a stainless steel plate with four screws was implanted into the cervical spine to help support my neck.

Post-surgery, I lay on the table and slowly opened my eyes. I could see the bright overhead lights. Dr. Baskin was waiting patiently for me to wake up. His operating gown was stained with blood. My blood.

He appeared exhausted, as though he had fought a major battle. The world famous Dr. Baskin smiled at me and shook his head.

"Nancy," he said. "It was worse than we thought. We don't really understand how you are still alive. You should be dead or at least a quadriplegic. Why you were spared is beyond our ability to understand."

Smiling inwardly I thought to myself, "No, my learned and kind doctor, even with all your studies and vast medical knowledge, you don't understand why I'm alive. But I do."

To this day, no medical expert understands how, or why, I am able to walk or use my arms and hands. They tell me I should be dead or paralyzed. They are all amazed that I am well, in excellent health, and completely pain free.

At each checkup during my recovery, I was always asked, "Are you sure you don't have any pain? And happily, I answered, "Not a flicker of pain anywhere."

That's right. The best doctors in the world said I should be dead. But I am not. People ask, "How did you do it? What is your secret? What gave you the power to overcome death?"

I don't blame these people. I know what happened to me seemed impossible. After all, who was I to escape death? Why didn't I die? There wasn't anything special about me.

I was just one ordinary woman alone in a city of over 6.6 million people, but I was rescued by Heaven.

Today I Am Happy and Healthy

It took me two years to recover from the accident and the Angel never left my side. He remained steadfast. Always near when I felt alone, all I had to do was ask with my mind, "Are you still here?"

And always, I heard his familiar voice reply, "I am here with you. Look to the future. See yourself healed. Just think about the future and don't think about today. Today is temporary. It will pass. You are going to be completely okay."

Oh, yes. There were days when the pain was almost unbearable. There were days when I became discouraged and cried myself to sleep at night. But each time my spirits fell down, the Angel picked me back up.

Every single day for two years he stayed by my side providing comfort and reassurance. My constant companion, I thought of him as my trusted friend.

Then one day, just as suddenly as the Angel appeared, he was gone. His job was over. I was as good as new.

My focus is different now than it was before the accident. I've learned to believe. Faith is a powerful thing. Faith saved my life when I had nowhere else to turn.

Today I expect to have what I desire because I believe in unlimited possibilities and hope. I've discovered what's really important in life. I've learned to trust the power of "The Invisible." And best of all, I feel deeply loved and protected by something greater than me.

Because I care about you, I am sharing my very personal story in case you are at a crossroads in your life and feel you have nowhere to turn, or you don't know what to do, or you feel utterly alone in the world.

I want you to know you are not alone. There are Angels in Heaven and on Earth who will help you just like they helped me.

Look at me. I am living proof that the "impossible" can happen. Imagine that.

I am alive because I cried out in the middle of the night, "Please help me!" And I was heard.

So don't ever think no one in Heaven will hear you, or that there are no such things as Angels. I had an Angel save my life in Houston, Texas, during the fall of 1997, at Methodist Hospital on Fannin Street.

You are not alone.

8

ANGELS ABOVE ME

"You cannot see me with your eyes,
but you know that I am there."

Angels above me
Angels below
Angels all around me
Wanting to know.

Are you happy?
Are you sad?
Are you worried?
Why are you mad?

Dear one,
Can't you see me?

Can't you feel me?
Don't you know?

I want to help you.
And love you.
And keep you from harm.

So honor me
By trusting me.
Please ask me for help.

When you're happy
I'm happy
And we both feel blessed.

Yes. Angels come to me
And walk with me.
They sleep in my bed.

I sense them.
I feel them.
I know they are near.
Their presence is comforting.
Their guidance is clear.

They're waiting to help me.
I just have to ask.
Whatever I need
They're up to the task.

Fretting and worrying
Does me no good.
When I trust in the Angels
Things work out as they should.

Thinking it over
It's easy to see
God's Angels in Heaven
Are watching over me.

9

TWITTERPATED

"Happy. Happy. Joy! Joy!"

Ever seen Bambi? Remember the part where he fell in love? His heart was rushing. His eyes grew wide and he couldn't stop staring at the beautiful fawn in front of him. "What is this strange feeling I feel?" he asked.

Thumper chuckled and replied, "Bambi, you are twitterpated!"

Bambi looked at Thumper in surprise and exclaimed, "Twitterpated must be dangerous. It is so powerful!"

And Thumper and all the animals in the forest had a good laugh … for they knew what twitterpated meant.

Perhaps you have been lucky enough to experience falling in love like Bambi. It has only happened to me once in my life and it was a powerful, exhilarating and fantastic experience. It's a feeling like no other.

Twitterpated is not just an ordinary type of love. Twitterpated knocks you off your feet so you can't think straight. All you know is you are so happy you don't know what to do with yourself.

Listen. A few years ago, I found myself completely and totally twitterpated. I don't know how it happened so fast, but it did. One day I was a completely rational adult; the next day I was behaving like the village idiot rambling on and on about how happy I was.

Not only was it exhilarating to be twitterpated, it was embarrassing to be acting like such a fool. But I didn't care.

Then, after months and months of going around with a silly grin on my face and acting stupid, I found myself thinking about my situation.

"I can't believe this is happening to me. I've lost my mind out of sheer happiness. Every time I think about the one I love, I get weak in the knees and a great big smile lights up my face. And when other people see me looking all goofy like that, they smile too. They understand what my silly face means.

They know I'm twitterpated!"

The whole twitterpated thing was amazing. I didn't know anyone could be so happy. All my life I've heard about being love-struck, head over heels in love, being on Cloud Nine.

Matter of fact, I remember Valentine's Day at elementary school. It was loads of fun because I got to exchange nice "I Love You" cards and eat cupcakes and heart-shaped candy. On that special day my Mom and Dad became all mushy and goo-goo eyed and they smiled at each other all day long.

So to me, being in love was a good thing that made people happy. I just didn't know how happy love could make a person! Being in love is a magical feeling. It's a joyous, rapturous, exquisite expression of happiness.

Smitten! Struck by a bolt of lightning! I'm twitterpated!

THREE LITTLE WORDS

*"My heart is overflowing
with great passion and love."*

*Do you know how very wonderful you are?
You are
Wonderful.*

*Do you realize how lucky I am
Just to know you?
I do.*

*I am grateful everyday
You are in my life.
Yes. You.*

In fact, I'm always saying to myself
Wow!
How did I get so lucky?

Did you know seeing you smile
Makes me smile too?
That's how important you are to me.

I can say "I love you" over and over again.
But three little words can't begin to tell you
How much you mean to me.

They are not enough words to describe
How proud I am of you
And the person you are.

It's impossible for mere words to describe
How beautiful you are
Inside and out.

After all, nothing can capture your essence
Your grace and compassion
Or your funny little laugh.

The way you light up a room
With just your presence
Is beyond description.

Words, just words,
Can't begin to describe how I feel
When I am with you.

I want you to know
You have made my life better
Just by being you.

You give me joy.
Did you know?
You make me happy.

You make my heart sing.
You make me want to dance.
In fact, you make me giggle all the time.

I want to shout it to the world.
I want to say it over and over again.
I love you!

11

YOU CAN DO ANYTHING

"Don't let the doubt win."

I was going fishing.

My father used to take me fishing when I was small. We never caught much of anything. We didn't even care. Catching something wasn't the point of going fishing for us. We just wanted to spend time together outside in nature's beauty.

Our fishing days together were happy days filled with lots of love and lots of my Dad saying to me, "Trust yourself. You can do it. You can do anything."

Those words meant I could climb a hill, catch a

fish, or do anything I set my mind to do. Even if I was worried about the mean kid across the street, or my flower that wouldn't grow, Dad always looked me straight in the eye and said in his calm, reassuring voice, "Trust yourself. You can do it. You can do anything."

Imagine how his words made me feel.

It didn't matter what I wanted to achieve. My father always said the same thing to me, "Trust yourself. You can do it. You can do anything."

There was power in my father's words. They helped me through times when I wasn't so sure of myself and was afraid to try. By saying those encouraging words over and over, he taught me to believe in myself, to step forward through fear and self-doubt.

Who knew words could be magical?

Unfortunately, as things happen sometimes, he died young and I was left without his love and words of support. No longer did I hear, "Trust yourself. You can do it. You can do anything."

When my Dad died, the magic died.

And as things happen sometimes, there were days when I no longer believed in myself. My inner strength would leave me. Fear would creep in on those scary days and leave me filled with self-doubt. Those kind of days were hard days. I would huddle up in a dark room and not go out, except for essentials. I wanted to cry all the time.

I was a mess after my dad died. My usual zest for life was gone. My mojo disappeared. I felt like I couldn't do anything right. I didn't trust myself anymore. Doubt overcame my every thought.

Usually I hid.

One day, I did what I had needed to do for a long time. I scheduled a day off. That special day had finally arrived. The whole day was mine and the anticipation of what lay ahead was delicious. Lucky me! I had twenty-four whole hours to do what I wanted to do.

Happily looking forward to the day ahead, I took pleasure packing each thing into the car. It was early morning, and the dew clung to the leaves outside.

How refreshing it was to be a part of the newness of an awakening day. How alive I was already beginning to feel. This was the first time I'd felt this good in a long time. A sense of adventure filled my being. It was an absolutely juicy feeling … the feeling of being totally alive.

I was going fishing today! I wondered what adventures lay ahead?

An owl called to me from the great swamp oak across the road. Happiness oozed thickly through my heart. I could smell the last of the night jasmine, which grew so abundantly. My footsteps crunched softly over the gravel, and again I heard my spirit chanting, "Yeah, yeah, yeah, I'm on my way to throw a line into the water. I'm going to take off my shoes and feel the soft muddy silt squeeze through my toes. I will grow drunk on the smell of the wildflowers."

Whether I caught a fish or not didn't matter. Just being outside in a beautiful place was good enough for me.

Lunch was packed with cold water, a crisp apple, and a peanut butter and jelly sandwich. The car trunk carried a brand new cane pole lovingly rigged the night before with a shiny new hook and a little brown cork.

I had all I really needed. After all, "I can do anything." Hmmm. I hadn't thought of those words in a long time.

Dawn had turned into morning by the time I arrived at the familiar place where I'd fished with my Dad long ago. Memories flooded my mind. It was good to be here in this place alone with my memories. In fact, it was wonderful. The water sparkled in the morning sun. My shoulders relaxed.

I felt alive and vibrant. It was a feeling I hadn't felt in what seemed like forever.

Gathering my things from the car, I walked toward the water and selected a place to sit down under an old oak tree. It was still here, I realized, the same tree my Dad and I sat under long ago.

I spread my blanket on the ground next to the tree and settled in. My lunch and cane pole lay on the blanket beside me. Taking a deep breath, I just sat there for a bit with my eyes closed in the cool shade of the lovely old oak tree.

How peaceful it was here.

Lost in memories of long ago, I heard my dad's laughter echo softly in the distance, and I was overwhelmed with a feeling of unconditional love. Suddenly I remembered something important my Dad had taught me. It was the healing power of gratitude.

All the things I was grateful for having in my life began to flood my mind. Remembering all the wonderful things in my life made me happy. How lucky I felt!

Feeling grateful and happy, my spirit immediately soared. My spirit felt uplifted. This happy, free feeling was so absolutely yummy. I was beginning to think maybe this was the way we were supposed to feel all the time. Grateful. Happy. Excited about life.

I reached over, picked up my fishing pole, and swung the line out across the water. The cork broke the surface of the smooth glassy water. Plop! Bull's eye. I hit my mark.

In the distance, doves cooed. I inhaled the mossy smell of the riverbank, and felt the sunlight soaking into my body. The breeze was lazy today. It stirred the branches of the trees above, and then gave up with a sigh.

Leaning back against the majestic old oak tree, I stretched my legs out and pushed off my shoes. Two bare feet and ten bare toes wriggled ecstatically. They were free.

Reaching downward toward the ground, I touched the dirt with my hand. Oh, it was cool—cooler than the air, and slightly moist too. I thought how dirt took on the smell of everything around it, such as minerals, and roots, and the plants growing and dying on its surface.

I remembered how much fun it was to make cookies out of dirt, grass, rocks, and water, how I loved squashing it all together with my hands, feeling the mud and grass squish between my fingers. I'd spend hours cheerfully patting out dirt cookies to bake in the afternoon sun.

The smell of the dirt I held in my hand reminded me of how much fun it was to play. Oh my! I couldn't remember the last time I had played and had fun. No wonder I was feeling bummed out. Not only had I forgotten the importance of being grateful, I'd forgotten how to play. Note to myself: Add play time to my calendar.

Oops! My cork moved. At least, I thought it did. It gave a bounce, but it was so quick. Now I was not sure if it moved or not.

I was probably so relaxed thinking about dirt that I didn't really see what happened. I must have been mistaken. I "just thought" I saw the cork move.

After all, I always screwed up everything. Stupid me. I could never get anything right.

It was amazing how at home I felt outside. It was like I was a part of everything in nature. It was like I counted for something and this little ladybug crawling on my jeans counted for something too. I hadn't seen a creature like this little ladybug in such a long time. In fact, I'd forgotten all about ladybugs.

I guess I hadn't spent much time outside in a while. Maybe that was another reason I'd been feeling out of sorts.

Looking up, I saw the sky and it was actually blue. I couldn't get over what I was seeing. The sky was actually bright blue. No yellow smog clouds here. Just white, soft, fluffy clouds floating in a brilliant blue sky.

Oh God, thank you. You thought of everything. Even fluffy clouds. Even ladybugs.

The cork moved again. Sitting up straight, I was determined to keep my eye on the cork this time. I was getting excited. My hands quickly tensed around the cane pole. Oh yes. The cork was definitely moving.

Watch out, fish! I am ready for you this time!

But the cork didn't move again. Determined to wait it out, I remained steadfast waiting for the cork to move.

I was beginning to feel like an idiot, sitting there, staring at that ugly cork, wondering if it would ever bounce up and down again. All I wanted was for that stupid cork to move. But, *nooooo.* The cork was dead still in the water.

There! I saw it move again. *Hmmm.* Maybe not.

Giving up, I leaned back against the tree and sighed. *Screw up. You're such a screw up.*

Finally, taut muscles throughout my body slowly began to relax. Anyway, it didn't really matter if the cork moved or not, did it? I was enjoying being here today. Anyway, Dad and I never cared if we caught a fish. We just enjoyed the journey.

Relaxed now, I lazily tossed the line and cork out into the water again. All the way down the cork sank and disappeared under the water with the weight of the hook, line and sinker. Then the little cork quickly popped back up on top of the water, and broke the surface tension.

Sitting alone in silence in this place of natural beauty, I realized I'd forgotten how to trust myself. I wasn't mistaken a while ago. That cork really did move a while ago. I saw it move.

Why? Why? Why?

Why did I doubt myself so often? Why didn't I trust what I knew to be true? What had happened to me that I couldn't believe what I saw and felt anymore? Where was my faith? Where was my confidence?

Honestly, I felt so alone sometimes, so disconnected, so ridiculous. I wondered if I was the only one who ever felt this way. Alone and scared and not sure of anything. That was me.

Hey, Cork, you are just like me. Did you know that? You're hollow on the inside, existing on the surface, just floating along with no direction in sight.

Hey Cork. What are you going to do about yourself?

But the cork was still.

Hey Cork. Why are you even here? Hey Cork. Do you recognize me? You should. I'm ordinary too.

But the cork was still.

Suddenly, the cork began to glide sideways ever so slowly. Then BAM! The cane pole was suddenly pulled downward. The line was taut.

My cork had been jerked beneath the water's surface and was completely out of sight now. Cork was gone!

Frantic, I jerked up on the bamboo pole. Cork, line, and hook now dangled above me. The bait on the hook was gone!

My mouth dropped open. I was stunned.

Proof I had seen the cork move now dangled before my eyes. The empty hook left no doubt a fish had nibbled at the bait causing the cork to move. I wasn't a screw up after all.

Standing there in awe, staring at the empty hook with eyes wide and an open mouth, I heard the magical words from long ago echo through my mind.

"Trust yourself. You can do it. You can do anything."

Years of self-doubt instantly evaporated. And just like that…my confidence was restored. I felt like my old self again … like I could do anything. My mojo was back!

I heard my Dad's soft laughter echoing through the trees once again. In his calm, and loving voice I distinctly heard him say, "I am with you always."

Immediately the heavy burden I had been carrying for so long was lifted off my shoulders as grief and fear of the unknown melted away. Death had not stolen my father from me. He was still watching over me … protecting me, loving me, encouraging me.

Imagine. Little did I know 24 hours earlier, my day off from work would become a major tipping point in my life. While talking to a small brown, fishing cork I grasped the full meaning of eternal life.

Love never dies.

Grateful, no longer do I feel depressed and angry. I feel happy and peaceful and loved. After all, I know I can do anything.

12

IN THE STILLNESS

"Knowingness is born in silence."

Be still.
Get quiet.
Relax.
Let go.

Listen.
Listen some more.
*What do you **hear**?*

Do you hear the knock at the door?
Has the tea kettle started whistling?
Is the music in the background too loud or too soft?
Did your inner voice speak to you?

Look all around you.
Look up.
Look down.
See *all the textures, shapes and colors.*
Isn't sight wonderful?

*What do you **feel**?*
Are you hot or cold?
Does your nose itch?
Is your clothing soft against your skin?

*Can you **smell** food being cooked?*
Is there perfume in the air?
Does the yellow rose in the garden have a scent?
Would food taste as good if you couldn't smell?

*Do you **sense** danger?*
Is the phone going to ring?
Did you follow your hunch today?
Do you sense money coming your way?
What does your intuition tell you?

Let me ask. Are you aware of each of your senses? Are you in touch with your body, mind and soul? Have you forgotten to take time for yourself? Are you numbed out?

Perhaps, day after day has gone by with you mechanically going through daily routines until one day, you wake up and notice you are in a rut. You realize you are not paying attention to your natural instincts. Not paying attention to what your heart is telling you. Not paying attention to your sixth sense.

When I realize I'm in a rut, I have to take action. I have no other choice. I have to do something different. I must change the pace a little; have a different environment; break the rut cycle.

Where I go to find myself again doesn't matter … as long it is quiet. Why do I require quiet to regain my strength?

I need to decompress without the constant stimulation and repetitive habit of my everyday life. I need to be still, observe the world around me, and pay attention to what my senses are telling me.

Frankly, I need to reconnect with my soul. I need the stillness to become me again. The real me.

New ideas unfold in the stillness as if by magic. Solutions to old problems appear out of nowhere. In stillness, I have light bulb moments of realization where solutions are suddenly so simple and clear.

After one of these light bulb moments I always find myself thinking the same thing, "Why didn't I think of this solution before? Why was this problem so hard for me to figure out? The answer to the problem is so simple."

The fact is this. I couldn't think of a solution to my problem before because I was bogged down with stress, pressure, noise, duties, repetition, demands, and environmental stimulation. Who can think in a hurricane? Certainly not me. I have to get out of that noisy rut.

Spending "alone time" outside in nature is one of my favorite things to do when I need to escape the dreaded rut. The beauty of nature reconnects me to my spirit. It reminds me I am a part of all that exists: the sky, the mountains, the trees, the wind. Yes, even God.

Picture it. My entire being is filled with awe, gratitude, and peace when I walk by the ocean, see a hummingbird, and listen to the waves wash ashore. Mindfulness becomes second nature and requires no effort or thought. The world blossoms around me as I am pulled into the natural beauty surrounding me. My grateful heart overflows with happiness. And what could be better than that--happiness?

In the stillness we become whole.
Go there ... to the stillness.
You will find yourself again

13

YOU DESERVE HAPPINESS

"I just want to be the Soul that I am."

Have you heard the old story about the elephant that had been chained to a post since he was baby?

Well, once upon a time this poor elephant was seized and taken into captivity. His owner kept him chained to a post and told him what to do. Day after day, the animal was brainwashed. He was controlled and told how to act and how to be. He was even told how to think.

Years went by and the elephant was always reminded each day that he was nothing but a dumb creature who deserved nothing. Imagine how his life was.

He was told what to think. He was told what he could do and what he couldn't do.

After many years, the owner went away and did not come back. Neighbors felt sorry for the poor beast. So they cut the chain that had kept him imprisoned all those years. Then the kind people stood back and waited for the elephant to claim his freedom…to be a free elephant…to be happy… to do what elephants do.

The neighbors waited and they waited. Nothing happened.

The elephant did not leave the post. He just stood there. He was even there the next day, and the next day, and the next day. He did not leave. There the great beast remained with his head down, standing next to the post where he had been chained most of his life.

The neighbors were stunned.

How could such a thing be? The elephant was no longer imprisoned by the chain around his leg. Yet he was still a prisoner.

Among the neighbors lived an old man who had seen many things. The years had made him wise. When the old man heard about the elephant who would not claim his freedom, the old man understood why the elephant remained as he was … a prisoner. He had seen the same thing happen before, not only among beasts, but among humans too.

The old man knew the elephant was imprisoned by the brainwashing from the past. There was still a voice in his head which said, "Who do you think you are? You are nothing. You do not deserve. Do what I say to do."

So although this magnificent creature was no longer physically chained, the elephant remained, standing by the post with his head down for the rest of his life, a prisoner of the voice from his past.

Happily, this is only a story.

Just recently a video went viral on the internet of an elephant which had actually had his chains cut and was set free after many years of cruel imprisonment.

The animal was so happy, he bellowed and trumpeted wildly. It was heart touching to see the freed elephant rejoice at receiving the right to be who he was … an elephant.

There is now a campaign to collect donations to help him remain free and independent for the rest of his life.

There is a moral to this story we can all learn from.

All creatures long to be free. They want to follow their own voice, achieve their own dreams, reach for the stars and hope for a better life. It's as simple as that.

If there is a voice from the past in your head controlling your life, it's time to set yourself free.

Cut the chains. Move away from the post of the past. Go forward and live your own dream. Your inner elephant will thank you.

14

LET YOUR SOUL SHINE

"Being who you really are sets you free."

I was told I couldn't.
So I couldn't.
Didn't.
Didn't even try.

I was told I didn't deserve.
So I accepted exactly that.
Nothing.

I was asked, "Who do you think you are?"
No reply came forth from my mouth.

*I just looked down at the floor
Because I didn't know who I was.*

*One day my eyes were opened.
I looked at things another way
And thought to myself
"Why not?"*

*Why not try?
Believe?
And accept what I deserve?*

*So I did try.
Believe.
And accept what I deserve.*

*My life changed in a remarkable way.
Everything was different.
Full of wonder and awe.*

*It happened the moment
I thought to myself,
"Why not?"*

*Today I listen to my own voice.
Not the voice of someone else.
Not the voice of fear.*

*My life overflows with excitement.
Hope.
Possibilities
And love.*

I am no longer asked,
"Who do you think you are?"
My presence says it all.

Free from the past,
I lift my arms to the sky
And shout for all the world to hear,
"Let your soul shine!"

15

THE WORKAHOLIC

*"When you are in your head,
it's hard to be in your heart."*

*Oh, hurry up and get it done.
Eat your breakfast on the run.
No time to smile.
No time to think.
No time to even stop and blink.*

*My shoulders droop.
My eyes feel strain.
I feel my life go down the drain.*

*Filled with tension
Filled with stress*

More coffee jitters
More duress.

More duress … more duress … more duress.
More stress … more stress … more stress
No time to rest …rest … rest.
Sigh

No!
It won't get done
Without my say
And it can't wait another day.

So hurry up and get it done.
Always up before the sun.
No time for rest.
No time for fun.

Don't waste my time.
Don't talk to me.
I only deal with work
And worry.

I know it all.
I do it best.
I'm more important
Than the rest.

Who am I?
I don't know.
I lost myself a long time ago.

16

A BALANCED LIFE

*"Those dates you have filled in on your calendar
are your life choices."*

We need balance in our lives.

Without balance in our thoughts, activities and relationships, people become disoriented and unhappy.
It's as simple as that.

When we are out of balance, we may not even
know why we are not satisfied. Not at peace. Rest-
less. We just know something is missing, but we don't
realize what that something is. Deep in our hearts we
sense a longing that won't go away.

Human beings become depressed when their lives are out of balance. Unhappiness creeps in and stakes a claim.

This often happens to workaholics and their families. As you can imagine, the whole family dynamic suffers when there is a workaholic in the family.

Lately, lack of balance created by workaholics has become a huge concern of mine because I am starting to see the devastating effects of overwork on people of all ages.

You see, not only have the families of workaholics been coming for readings, but workaholics, themselves, are coming for readings, too. They all feel lonely, like nobody cares about them at all. Workaholics create an environment of isolation.

Amazingly, every person in the family has arrived for their reading with the same emptiness in his or her heart. Each person has felt depressed. Many have sat in front of me and cried. These poor people intuitively sensed that something was missing in their lives, but most of them didn't know what it was. They didn't realize how far out of balance their lives had become.

You see, their world revolved around work. There was no pleasure, no fun, no family time. Just work.

Unfortunately, many of the workaholics didn't seek my help until their world had completely fallen apart. Because work had become so all-consuming, they were usually the last ones in the family to realize something was wrong.

Let me be clear here. There is a difference between working hard and being a workaholic. There are many hard-working people who are not workaholics. Hard-working people continue to take time off for vacations, health needs, spirituality, and their family. Most of these hardworking people are happy and satisfied. They lead good lives. They feel fulfilled. These people work hard, but they find time for everything else in life, too. Their lives are in balance. They are happy.

A workaholic can never have enough, be enough, or do enough.

These are fear-driven people who are obsessed with work. They can't get enough of anything, so these people are never satisfied.

Wikipedia defines a workaholic as a person who is addicted to work.

As you know, there is a price to pay for addiction of any kind. The stress of overwork produces adrenaline in the body. Adrenaline produces a kind of high. Workaholics become adrenaline junkies who wear their bodies out with stress. Workaholics push and push themselves because they believe they must work to have "value."

Not only are they self-absorbed perfectionists, they are impatient, compulsive people. They are hard to get along with, probably because they are always stressed out, tired, and overworked.

Extreme workaholics are usually narcissists. There is no room, or time, for anything outside of work in the life of a workaholic. These people are totally out of balance.

I recently did a reading for a man whose life had been shattered by his addiction to work. The poor man had not only lost himself, but he had lost those he loved.

He came to see me because he couldn't understand why his wife had left him. Not only was he depressed over losing his family, the stress of overworking had caused his health to suffer.

Please understand this was a kind man, a loving man. He wasn't a monster. He simply had no way of evaluating his own worth unless it had a dollar sign attached to it.

In his worldview, he was showing love to his family by "providing" for them. What he didn't realize was that providing for your family goes far beyond the things that money can buy.

The Japanese recognize that workaholics have a serious problem which can lead to early death. Yes, it's true. People can literally work themselves to death.

So please, my Friend, if you know someone who has completely lost themselves in their work, especially to the exclusion of finding time for friends, family, and their health, try to help them as best you can.

They may have simply forgotten how much they are missing in life and just need a gentle reminder.

We all get lost sometimes and need a friend to show us the way.

17

TODAY YOU WHISPERED

"Since I live in your heart, you can always find me."

Today I heard a whisper in the background.

It was the sound of a voice, a quiet voice, which seemed to emerge from deep within me. I don't know exactly where the voice came from. I just know it was there, inside me, with an urgency and beckoning whisper that could not be ignored.

Once again, you were trying to tell me something.

Although I recognized your voice and I knew what you wanted, I pretended I did not hear you.

I pretended I did not know you. And yes. I even pretended you were not real.

I even said to you, "Go away! Leave me alone." But you would not.

This time was different than all the other times you spoke to me. Yes. This time when you whispered, you were more insistent than ever before to be heard. In fact, I could sense you actually pushing at my body and trying to make me listen.

I don't know how you pulled that off, but you did. At first it was a gentle nudge somewhat like a little child tugging at their mother to do something.

That's right. I wouldn't tell anyone else this, but I actually sensed you pulling at me. Let's just say it was an "implied suggestion" resembling a nudge. You might call it an impression of being nudged. Impression or not, the experience was about as real as you can get and I knew it.

But you know what I did?

I ignored you like I always did. Even though the urgency and the insistence to be heard was very real, I simply shut myself off and refused to listen to you. "Go away!" I said once again, "You can't be real. Leave me alone!"

And suddenly, just like that, you went away. You did as I asked. Then I was sorry. Really sorry.

I wondered where you went. I wondered if maybe I had made a mistake sending you away. And believe it or not, I even wondered if maybe I should have listened to what you had to say. I couldn't stop thinking, "Maybe I should have listened."

I began to feel regret. Then I felt despair deep within. Somehow I knew I had made a mistake demanding that you go away. The thought of never hearing your voice again flooded over me and I was filled with sadness. It felt like something important had been lost.

But you weren't gone for long.

Out of nowhere, and very unexpectedly, there you were again deep within the recesses of my mind and my heart. It was like you were a part of me … like you were me … like you couldn't go away even if you tried.

Happy that you had not abandoned me, I spoke to you out loud.

"Oh, please help me understand what is going on. Tell me who you are. I know you are not my mind or my heart. I know you are different. I've always sensed that you were different. I don't know how I know, but somehow I understand that you are different from my brain and my emotions."

It feels like you are your own person … with your own voice … a voice you use to talk to me.

Most of the time you speak to me in a soft whisper from somewhere in the back of my mind; but it's not like that this time. No, not this time.

Your voice didn't sound far away like it did before. This time you were not so quiet. Neither were you subtle. This time you were not gentle. No. This time you were pulling at me."

Finally, I absolutely understood that you would not stop and leave me alone until I did as you asked. So I did as you wanted. I had no choice.

Listening to you was very hard for me to do, because I had to step out of my comfort zone. And stepping out of my comfort zone meant I had no place to hide anymore. I had to make myself vulnerable. Oh no. Oh no. Oh no. I could no longer just play it safe.

I had to do as you wanted or risk being without you. And somehow, being without you was a thought I just couldn't bear. So, reluctantly, I did as you asked.

"Okay," I said. "I'm going to listen to what you have to say even though it's scary for me."

All the while, I was muttering to myself, "You've chosen the wrong person. I must be hearing things. This isn't really happening to me. It must be a thought and not a separate voice I hear. I wish you would just go away because you scare me.

No. Don't leave. I don't really want you to go away. I don't want to be without you. Not really. When I thought you went away, it made me sad. I missed you."

The voice inside me saw that I was listening and knew it finally had my full attention.

The moment of truth had arrived. Time stood still in the deafening silence. Off in the distance I heard the familiar voice whisper to me. And this is what I heard:

"Do this thing. Listen to my voice which guides you. Start now.

If you send me away, I'll just come back. Without me, you won't rest and be happy. No. You'll be thinking about me and wondering what I wanted to tell you.

You will be wondering why you didn't listen and how in the world you could be such a scared chicken. Oh yeah. Then you will be searching for me and you will be sorry I'm gone."

So I did what the voice wanted. I decided to listen.

Oh yes. I gathered up my courage, even though my heart was pounding so hard and fast I thought everyone around me could surely hear it beating.

Surprisingly, I actually put aside my disbelief and skepticism.

This time, I didn't say to myself that you weren't real. This time, I wasn't embarrassed or self-conscious or doubtful about anything. I didn't hide. I didn't argue. I just listened to what you had to say without judgment.

It was phenomenal! It was an awakening. Suddenly, there you were. I felt you, I sensed you, and I knew you were really real. You weren't some figment of my imagination. You were you. The voice inside me.

Acknowledging your presence was surreal. Yet, it was the most real moment of my life.

Instantly, I understood you were distinctly different than me. You were separate from me. Your voice was your own voice and not just a thought in my head. You presence was your presence; not that of someone else; certainly not the voice of my human self.

You were your own form of energy.

Astonished, I realized I had never known you at all. In fact, it was the other way around. It was you who knew me. You were the observer … the wise one.

O.M.G. What a realization! It was you who knew me. You even loved me. I knew that now. I felt it. You actually loved me.

In this extraordinary moment of understanding, I was flabbergasted at how much I didn't know, what I had to learn, and what greatness exists in an invisible world that we don't see, much less understand.

Today you whispered. But this time, I didn't say, "Go away." This time, all I could say was, "Thank you for not leaving me."

18

TRUSTING THAT LITTLE VOICE

*"The hidden factor in all great outcomes
is intuition."*

Have you ever wondered what your life would be like if you listened to your intuition? If you paid attention to that big hunch? If you stayed away from people and places that "didn't feel right."

Would your life be different?

Do you ignore that little voice inside you? What about those crystal clear *knowings* you sometimes have? Can you sense when there is danger on the road ahead? Have you ever known when the phone was going to ring?

Each and every one of us is born to be aware of our environment. Just like other animals on earth, humans are also born with natural abilities to protect themselves from harm. These protective abilities, called senses, are known as: sight, touch, smell, hearing, taste, and intuition.

Intuition is our sixth sense. For example, that still small voice in your head, the feeling that won't go away, your strong hunch, the knowingness that insists it is right, an urgent feeling that you must act now are all examples of human intuition at work.

Animals pay attention to their senses to help them survive. For instance, dolphins and bats use echolocation to help guide them through unfamiliar or unseen territory. Echolocation is an intuitive form of radar and sonar. Migrating birds, whales, and butterflies follow intuitive homing instincts to return to the same location every year to reproduce their species.

We human animals have our intuition to watch over us. Not only can it help protect us, intuition can help us prosper in so many ways that it is hard to name all the ways.

Paying attention to what your intuition is telling you can pay off big time.

Oprah Winfrey, Thomas Edison, Steve Jobs, and Einstein all paid attention to their intuition and look where it got them.

Hey. I love you.

But, I bet you already sensed that.

19

IT ISN'T EASY BEING ME TODAY

"At one time or another we have all been a little lost.
So don't cast any stones."

I don't know why
You had to fall in love with her
When you had me loving you at home.

You are my husband.
You are their dad.
Our family's been pulled apart
By the lust in your heart.

It isn't easy being me today.

Seeing eyes staring as I pass by
And wondering if they know,
You told me last night
That you don't love me anymore.

Life's been hard
Knowing you were kissing her.
Wanting her.
Holding her so tight.

How can a heart hurt so bad
That you want to lie down and die?
You are my husband and you are their dad.

I look at your picture and I wonder why
It's come to this.
You don't love me anymore.

It isn't easy being me today.

20

LOST LOVE

*"Try looking at things from a different perspective.
You might find a better point of view."*

Like any growing and evolving creation on this planet, we thrive when certain conditions are met. We need food. We need water. We need air. But there is something else we need. Without it, we die. Can you guess what I'm talking about?

It's love.

Bless its heart, love is the most misunderstood emotion of all. We understand hate. Hate makes people feel powerful and "right." Anger is a little scarier because we worry anger might start driving the car for us. Lust is easy to understand. Lust wants what it wants and refuses to listen to reason. It's sexy, and in its way, as deceptive as hate because it makes people feel temporarily powerful. So what about romantic love?

A man falls in love with a woman, let's say, not because she is "deserving" of his love or has personal merit, but because she makes him feel wonderful about himself. She holds up a mirror, and he falls in love with his own idealized reflection. Then he ends up needing her to continue showing him his beauty and perfection so he can feel good about himself. Does that give his love less nobility and value?

Like most things in life, the answer is more complicated than that.

When we fall in love, we have stars in our eyes. We see the beloved as exotic and Other and beautiful. We blind ourselves to the other person's faults. We even make their faults "adorable" and yet further evidence of their perfection.

The reason we love to be in love is because there is no resistance. None. All positive emotion flows in a single direction with nothing to obstruct it.

Think of a river. A river can't flow in two directions at once. It simply flows without effort. When it comes across a boulder, it flows around it. The only thing that stops a river is a dam.

Sometimes, we are the dam.

We stop the flow of love when we start focusing on what we don't like and stop focusing on what we do like. Once the flow of love stops, the energy in the relationship changes. And that once lovely river comes to a standstill. It has been artificially stopped. Love dies.

We must remember … We are the perfection that we see in the Beloved, and that the Beloved sees in us. The best of us doesn't go away just because the Beloved no longer sees it.

Let's face it. Lost love hurts. Sometimes we think we will never get over a breakup. Many people go through a mourning process and experience actual grief when a love affair is over. It is natural to feel a sense of loss. Something precious has been lost … love.

As in any kind of grief, your loss should be felt and experienced so healing can place. Be kind to you. You have suffered a loss. Allow yourself time to heal.

It's going to get better. I promise.

21

THERE IS A REASON
FOR EVERYTHING

*"No matter what your circumstances, you have the
wisdom within you to lead you to happiness."*

I was alone on an island of remarkable beauty.

It was a difficult time in my life. I was awash in the
grief of a failing marriage. At first, even the glorious
beauty of the island seemed as though it were mock-
ing me. As I sat and listened to the murmuring of the
waves, my heart was just breaking and I wondered if I
would ever be happy. I wondered if I could ever trust
love again.

Overwhelmed, not only didn't I know what I was going to do, I didn't know who I even was.

I watched the sandpipers delicately pick their way over the sand. At sunset, when the water rushed to the shore and the sand looked like sheeted glass, I felt as though I alone were to blame for the failure of my marriage. What had I done wrong? Maybe I was defective, or worse—unlovable.

My sister and I had planned this vacation for months. The first week of our three week Hawaiian holiday had started out so nicely. No cell phones, no computers, just sisters who were best friends.

The first week was spent in Lanikai on the island of Oahu. Every day we lay on the picturesque beach, laughing and talking and catching up on old times. We felt like young girls again. We giggled, acted silly and relaxed. Together, we dined under the stars and wore fragrant flowers in our hair. We were happy, and heaven knew we both needed a little happiness at that time in our lives.

All too soon the first week of our vacation was over and we left Oahu to spend the second week of our vacation on the island of Maui.

Luck was with us when we checked in at the hotel in Maui. We were upgraded to a magnificent two-bedroom suite overlooking the water. Excitedly, we each claimed a bedroom and began to unpack.

We had just finished unpacking our suitcase when the phone in our room rang. It was one of those calls no one wants to get.

My sister's husband had suffered a heart attack.

Frantically, my sister threw her clothes back into her suitcase and caught the next flight back home. She hid tear-swollen eyes behind dark sunglasses, choked back sobs, and boarded the airplane wondering if she would make it home in time.

I worried. I cried. I prayed for both of them. Each time I walked by her empty bedroom, my heart gave a painful lurch. I felt more alone, depressed, and helpless than ever before. There was nothing I could do to help them.

After three days of moping around, I realized that I had begun feeling sorry for me, too.

I couldn't bear my self-pity. But what was I going to do all by myself in a tropical paradise full of newlyweds and young families?

I left Maui and flew to the last island on our vacation itinerary, the Big Island of Hawaii. When I arrived in Kona, I decided to rent a car. For hours, I drove along the isolated coast line of the Big Island of Hawaii. Only one car passed me on the deserted highway. It was me, the road, and the vast open sea below.

Like many women, I had worked too hard, taken care of everyone but me, and kept postponing the things I wanted to experience. I wasn't living my life; I was living everyone else's life. In fact, I wasn't a human being. I was a human doing. I had become a tourist in my own life seeing to everyone else's needs and none of my own.

But I didn't know yet how far down the rabbit hole I had fallen.

The hours slipped by as I drove along the coast. Clouds of scarlet and gold and royal purple crowned the setting sun. I needed to reach my destination soon to rest and eat and sleep. About half a mile off the road, I came to a tiny village of ramshackle condominiums. The condos were old and not so ritzy anymore. There wasn't any air-conditioning, television, phones, or Internet. And there were very few guests, mostly people on their way to Kona.

What a disappointment. When I reserved the place online, it sure didn't look like that. In the online photos, the condos appeared new and fresh and upscale. I hadn't hesitated to book for the entire week.

Online, the condos had a unique appeal to them. They radiated an energy that said, "I am what you are seeking." Needless to say, I felt powerfully drawn to them, like they had an amazing secret to share, something I needed, something very special.

I couldn't believe my eyes when I first saw my dingy room!

I had traveled a long way. I was alone, scared, and felt isolated on this sparsely-populated island. Visions of the Bates Motel were now flashing through my mind. But night had fallen, and there wasn't anything I could do since my accommodations were out in the middle of nowhere. I didn't have much choice but to spend the night.

That's when I fell apart. I couldn't take it anymore. Nothing in my life was working out for me. Not my relationships, not my "soul refreshing" holiday. Nothing. I sat down and cried.

I repeated over and over to myself how I didn't deserve this. My sister and brother-in-law didn't deserve this. My marriage was over, and I didn't know which way to turn. I didn't know who I was anymore.

I was lost in the middle of nowhere. A failure. A horrible person. A loser.

Exhausted, I crawled into bed and sobbed myself to sleep. Little did I know I was about to learn an important life lesson.

There is a reason for everything.

The next morning when I woke up, I discovered to my surprise that I hadn't been murdered in the night. I ventured into the kitchen and made a fresh cup of Hawaiian coffee. Then I went out on the lanai to watch the sun rise over the ocean.

I could see the water glittering in the near distance.

Above it, rising from the ocean, the sun commanded the morning sky. Rays of crimson, neon pink and antique gold chased the night away. The grounds stretching before me were lush and green. Frangipani perfumed the air, and orchids nodded in the warm breeze. Hummingbirds dipped their slender beaks inside the rainbow-colored throats of a hundred tropical flowers.

Immersed in the glory of the radiant morning, my grumpy, "Woe is me" mood melted away. I knew I had arrived in Eden.

The isolation of the place forced me to slow down and relax. The beauty of the island brought me peace.

Each day I walked barefoot on volcanic sand that was the color of jet black pearls. I listened to the waves and gazed out over the vast, eternal ocean.

I read inspiring books. I dozed. I drank milk out of coconuts. Each morning, I walked down to bask in the sun on the deserted black sand beach, which was a haven for sea turtles. Slow and plodding on land, the turtles turned quick and playful in the ocean. Many mornings, I joined in and frolicked beside them in the blue water. When we grew tired, we swam to shore and lay on the warm sand.

Except for a few locals, I was often alone on the beach. I wasn't distracted by technology, a knock on the door, or a "to do" list.

Solitude had been forced upon me. There was nothing else to do but BE.

Amazingly, I began to feel as though I had come back into alignment with something that had always been there, patiently waiting, hoping I would find it again. This part of me wasn't sad or alone. It was vibrant and alive.

One sunny morning, in a flash of complete understanding, I realized an essential truth about my identity. I liked who I was.

Funny, I had never known that before. It was quite a surprise to discover I was actually an okay person--even likeable--even lovable. When I thought about who I was as a person, my values and beliefs, I immediately stood a little taller and held my head a little higher. There was sureness in my step that wasn't there before.

Much to my amazement and delight, I discovered I was proud of the woman I had turned out to be. I was okay after all. I wasn't a loser. I was a really nice woman.

Spirit renewed, filled with hope and direction, I knew I was going to be alright, no matter what happened.

Alone in the middle of nowhere, at a time when I felt beaten and lost, I discovered what I had been searching for my whole life. Myself.

There really is a reason for everything.

22

WHEN BAD THINGS HAPPEN

"Tomorrow always brings us another chance.
So hang on for tomorrow."

You get depressed.
You cry.
You get mad at yourself.
You get mad at God.

You look up toward Heaven.
You thrust your fist in the air
And shout,
"There is no God!"

It's okay for you to feel this way.
Everybody has felt this way
At one time or another.

God understands us.
Our grief.
Our anger.
Our disappointment
When things don't go the way we want.

God has these feelings too.

So if something really bad happens to you,
Go ahead.
Cry and cuss.
Get mad and grieve.

Then after you are through,
Look around and notice
That at the same time the bad thing is happening
There is also something good happening in your life.

When things get tough,
The important thing to remember is
Everything happens for a reason.

We may never understand
What the reason is
Until later.

MAGIC ON THE HORIZON

"Good job, God!"

Science tells us everything is made of energy. Every. Single. Solitary. Thing.

Picture it.

The grass beneath your bare feet, infinite varieties of bark, leaves that interpret the joy and longing of the winds that blow through them, meaty puppy breath, even a human or a red tractor are all a form of energy.

And if all energy on earth were reduced down to its smallest part, everything that exists would blend together into one thing. And so it is.

Essentially, we are one with all that exists, including our Creator. Amazing isn't it? We are one with all. For this reason we are naturally drawn to the vast beauty of the great outdoors.

Nature is a part of who, and what, we are.

Taking a walk, hiking in the mountains, and strolling alongside the ocean automatically puts us in a Zen-like state of mind. It's an indescribable feeling of awe and wholeness which encompasses our heart and soul.

When we are outside in nature, we are filled with a deep knowingness that everything is as it should be. Being in nature, we feel we have come home. We feel we have come home because essentially we have.

In search of this peaceful feeling of relaxation and calm, in search of our roots, the majority of people are naturally drawn to the sea. Scientists tell us the sea is where we come from. Our hearts tell us tell us more or less the same thing. Our souls tell us even more.

We can't take our eyes off the sparkling water.

We vacation and honeymoon on the ocean. The price of oceanfront property skyrockets in comparison to property with no ocean view. Everyone, it seems, wants to be near the water. In fact, if you look at maps showing where most people live in the world, you will find the highest concentration of people living along sea coasts.

Without question, the sea is magical. It draws us to it. It nourishes our soul. Basking in the warm sunlight, we feel peaceful and relaxed. Gazing at the horizon, we find ourselves relaxed, drifting into a trance-like state.

It is hard to remember who we are, I know. It is hard for most of us to disconnect from electronic communications and the busyness of this world to actually commune with Nature.

But the Earth itself is the thing that will make us happy and well. In the beauty of the great outdoors we discover we are one with all that is … ever was … and ever will be.

ONE MISTY MORNING

"You are loved beyond imagination."

Soft mist settles
Along the horizon of sea and space.
Water and sky melt into one.

Sitting silently
Basking in the warmth of the sun
Rays of light softly fall
Across my face and shoulders.

My innermost self is comforted
Soothed
And peaceful.

I lift my face upward
To soak in the warm sun
And hear myself softly say
"Ahhhh, this is wonderful."

My very Being has been drawn
Into the splendor
Of this magical Monet moment.

A never-ending,
Ever-present horizon
Has captivated my Soul.

Filled with quiet joy and peace
I am.
And that is just the way it is.

Misty, water colored hues
Of blue, pink and violet
Lay across the sparkling, sunlit water.

Magical pastels of color
Offering hope and acceptance
For the very likes of me.

What?
Me?
Are you sure?
Oh, my God.

Filled with reverence and awe
I take a deep breath of realization
Yes. Me.

Overwhelmed at the thought
A tear slips from my eye
And glides down my warm cheek.

My heart smiles.
For I am humbled
And deeply grateful.

I am accepted
Just as I am.
Imagine that.

Something worthwhile
Beyond the very likes of me.
Cares about me.

With great emotion welling up inside
I feel overcome with the realization
I am loved beyond all imagination.

Relaxed and at peace
In this beautiful Monet moment
Of earth, sea, and sky flowing into one
I know who I am.

I am the sky.
The wind.
The sea.
And the cloudy mist of the horizon.

I am part of all that is.

It is wonderful!
This feeling.
This knowing.
This oneness.

My soul lingers in space.
Suspended in time.
Suspended.
In time.

Spellbound.
Blessed.
Happily aglow
With love for ALL.

I find myself in awe
Of the beauty
That is ours
For free.

The only cost is a moment of our time
To pause
And gaze upon the horizon
Where water and sky melt into one.

A PARENT'S LOVE

"Kids are wonderful. They don't go around saying, 'Prove it to me.' They say, 'Wow!'"

When I was a little girl I had a mutt named Lady.

Lady could do anything. At least I thought she could.

She would run and chase me all day, and she went on adventure walks with me to hunt wild blackberries. When I finally tired myself out playing, Lady would lay down next to me while I napped.

As you might have already guessed, I loved Lady. And like most kids, I thought my dog was the greatest dog ever. Secretly, I thought she was Super Dog. All she needed was a little cape.

Everyone knew how I felt about Lady. I loved that little black and white mutt dog with all my heart.

However, my dog wasn't the only one I loved. I loved my Mom and Dad very much too. Dad was an absolute hero in my eyes. He even let me stand on top of his feet as we danced around the living room. He taught me how to hammer a nail, and he taught me how to find the good in every person I saw.

So I decided to marry him when I grew up. When anybody asked me who I was going to marry, I always said, "Daddy."

Time passed, as it does, and it wasn't long before I was no longer a child. One day I fell in love and got married. I had a home of my own and a husband to love. Plus, I had my mother and father and my brother and sister to love. And believe it or not, Lady was still around for me to love, too.

Since I had so many people and one dog to love, there were so many different ways for me to express love. So naturally, I thought I knew everything there was to know about all the different kinds of love that existed.

But then my son was born.

Surprisingly, my love for that little baby boy was unlike any other kind of love I had ever felt before. In fact, the love I had for him was all encompassing. It was a special kind of love. It was a parent's love.

I was so happy I thought my heart would burst with pure joy! The love I felt for my baby boy was so strong at times, it was truly overwhelming. I had never, ever, felt that kind of love before. It was a gentle love, but a fierce and powerful love too. It was a Mother's love.

Holding my baby son in my arms, looking into his big wondering eyes, I knew I would do whatever it took to protect him. For the rest of my life, his wellbeing would be foremost in my life.

Five years later, a little girl arrived who laughed and giggled all day long. She was born on my birthday and I felt blessed once more. Two beautiful children were mine to love now.

How wonderful life had become for me. It was filled with laughter, giggles, questions, lots of cuddles, and dogs and cats, too. Oh yes, and a bunny rabbit.

But then, one day, just when I thought I had experienced every single kind of love there was in the world, something absolutely wonderful happened to me. I learned I would be a grandparent.

Memories flooded my mind of days gone by. I remembered holding my own little babies in my arms and how much love I felt for them. Each time I looked into their beautiful face, or noticed the dimples in their little hands, my heart would overflow with pure happiness. It was a good time, a happy time, a blessed time.

Babies aren't called "bundles of joy" for nothing.

There is something wonderfully different about the love a parent has for his or her child. This special kind of love is so indescribable it must be felt within a parent's heart to be truly understood.

The song, "Sunrise, Sunset" from *Fiddler on the Roof* captures the love of a parent for their child. I get tears in my eyes each time it is sung because I am instantly pulled back into the memories of being a young mother. My heart overflows with love for my children as I sit in the darkness of the audience weeping.

"Sunrise. Sunset. Swiftly go the years." How true the lyrics are. Many sunrises and sunsets have swiftly gone by in my life. My two babies are grown now.

Once again, I've been blessed with a brand new kind of love: a grandparent's love for their grandbaby.

So in honor of the birth of my grandson, Liam, and all new parents around the world, the following poem was written just for you…those who love deeply.

This is a special time, filled with a special love, unlike any love you will ever know.

26

DO YOU KNOW HOW MUCH
I LOVE YOU?

*"There is a reason Heaven picked you
to be here now."*

*I see your face and stroke your hair.
I feel the warmth of your small body
Nestled next to mine.*

*A deep sense of contentment wells up inside me.
The dream I longed for is here
Sleeping in my arms.*

Soft baby breath brushes across my skin.
Time stands still
As we silently blend into one.

Suspended in time
Blissfully happy
This moment feels surreal.

Yet, I see you
And touch you.
I hear your soft sigh.

My heart is filled with joy.
I know I've been blessed.
A tear glides down my cheek.

Silently rejoicing
Humbly in awe
I am grateful you are mine.

Do you know how much I love you?
Somehow
I think you do.

I'm so happy
I want to sing and dance
And lift my arms to the sky.

I want to shout out loud
At the top of my voice
"Thank you, God!"

Then I remember
The days will go by
As days do.

One day
You'll grow up
And go away.

Closing my eyes
Shutting out the future
I give thanks for this time we have together.

You are my baby.
My precious.
My dream come true.

Do you know how much I love you?
Somehow
I think you do.

27

ONCE THERE WAS NOTHING

"When you were born,
Heaven wept tears of pure joy."

Did you know that once there was nothing?

Yes. That's right. There was absolutely nothing. There were no oceans, or trees, or even stars in the sky. Actually there was not even a universe. Imagine that … absolutely nothing. It's hard to do. Isn't it?

Nothing means there wasn't a sound, or a breeze, or even light. Yes. It was completely dark … because there was nothing.

There were no worms, or bull dozers, or the oldest thing in the world because there was no world. That's right.

Just think about it. There was no Great Sphinx of Egypt. And believe it or not, you couldn't even find a sand dollar on the beach, because there was no beach.

This place called Nothing was just that … nothing.

Nothing was a very lonely, boring, dull place. It was almost scary. After all, absolutely nothing is kind of scary. Don't you think?

But most of all, the worst thing about Nothing, is that Nothing had no feelings. None at all. So that's why Nothing was such a dull, boring, lonely place. It was a place where there were absolutely no feelings.

You see, way back then, and once upon a time, that is just the way it was. There really was nothing … nothing at all. It's hard to imagine, isn't it?

But, then it happened.

Out of nowhere and total nothingness, a tiny, little spark of light appeared. It was so small that it could hardly be seen at all. In fact, if there had been a microscope during the time of nothingness, the little speck of light would be almost invisible.

Oh, yes, the tiny light was very hard to see. But make no mistake about it, that teeny bit of light was there. And there it remained; steadfast, shining its tiny beam of light out into the darkness of nothing.

It was all there was in the vast emptiness. Just one little spark of light, all alone, in utter and complete darkness.

But, no matter how little it was, it was there.

Now, even though the light was very small, so small it was almost invisible, the tiny speck of light was a mighty, powerful thing. After all, it had appeared out of nowhere in a place where there was nothing.

Astounding, isn't it? In fact, the thought of such a thing happening is a bit overwhelming. Why would anything want to come to such a dark, empty place as Nothing?

The little light arrived by choice. You see, it had a very important job to do. It was to become a beacon of light in the darkness signaling what was to come.

As time went by, the little light continued to shine forth light offering a ray of hope in the darkness. And the place called Nothing now held hope and promise.

Yes. There was light. And there was hope. There was promise. And it was mighty. And it was good. So much better than it was before when there was absolutely nothing.

But after a while, the little light became lonely, and wanted more light to hang out with. You see, the little light had a lot of love to share.

So the little light began to wish for what it wanted most…love. And as the light wished, and wished, and wished some more, the little light began to grow and grow, and shine even brighter.

And you know what happened then?

The light wished for love so hard…a star was created out of nothingness just like that. And the new star was beautiful. In fact, it was glorious!

The little light smiled real big and declared, "Wow! This is good."

Matter of fact, the new star was so magnificent, and extraordinary, that it needed a special name of its own. So the tiny light looked at its first creation, created from love and named it Love.

And the place of Nothing could never be called Nothing ever again. No. Not ever. Because now there was light, hope, promise, beauty and most of all, there was Love.

And the little light was filled with happiness. In fact, it loved the star named Love so much, that joy came to be. Yes. Complete and total joy came to be because of pure happiness.

It was incredible. All by itself, the little light had created a place which had feelings. And as you know, feelings are a mighty big thing.

More and more time went by. And the star named Love remained shining out into the darkness, along with the little light which created it.

Hope, light, promise, love, joy, and happiness radiated out into darkness. And it was good. In fact, the whole thing was absolutely wonderful.

Amazing rays of brilliant light danced on the star's surface. Shooting flames flew outward into space. The star named Love glowed with brilliant colors of white, and red, and orange, and gold.

As the flames jumped forth from the core of the new star, they produced something new in the place called Nothing. It was called noise. In fact, if you were close enough, you could actually hear all the popping, crackling and sizzling going on. The Star of Love sparkled and glowed and made funny noises.

On, and on, and on, one sparkle after another, the new star glittered in the darkness. It radiated so much light, that it warmed the cold, frigid darkness of space. Thank goodness.

Once where there was utter silence, the Star named Love produced sound. Sparkle, crackle, roar!

More time passed and eventually the little light started to wish for more company to share its love with.

And guess what? All that wishing, from that mighty little light, stirred up creation again. And boom! Just like that, another particle of light came into being. It was a really, really little bit of light. But it was there, another star.

Suddenly, one by one, more and more stars were created out of sheer joy. The whole thing was totally amazing. Picture how it must have looked when lots of stars started popping up everywhere in the black, black darkness of empty space.

The little light was so pleased with all the new stars that something big was bound to happen again. And it did. Creativity suddenly exploded in one huge, gigantic burst of creation!

Oh, yes. All at once giant suns came to be. Planets came to be too. Even whole galaxies were formed. All at once. And of course, while all that was going on, The Milky Way was born and began spilling more glittering, sparkling light all over the place.

Wow.... Can you imagine? Whole universes, suns, and moons and even the majestic Milky Way were created by a single moment of pure joy.

The darkness was now filled with all kinds of light. There were beautiful clusters of stars, soft glowing moons, and whole universes filled with planets.

And the little light was so happy. It danced up and down and said, "Good golly, Miss Molly! This is super good."

And so it was. Brand new skies, in many new universes, had been filled with light, love, sound, promise, hope and joy. And that was a really big deal. Because remember, once there was absolutely nothing.

The whole happening was so absolutely wonderful, that the little light was completely overcome with love. There was love everywhere. More love than ever before. In fact, the little light was totally surrounded by love.

And in that very special, single magical moment filled with so much joyful love, the most magnificent creation ever created was born.

It was filled with the light of its creator, and had totally awesome love to share. It was so glorious; it was the most beautiful creation of all time.

And the little light rejoiced as never before, and the skies in all the universes rejoiced too. Even the majestic Milky Way was thrilled. And as you can imagine, the Star named Love cried tears of pure happiness.

So beloved the new creation was by all of the rest of creation … it was named Precious.

Precious was not a star, or a moon, or a great river. It was even more magnificent than any of these things. It was more rare than a galaxy or a comet.

Precious could not be replaced; for there was only one. Anywhere. And to top it off, Precious was the hope for the future, and all good things that will come tomorrow.

Oh my gosh! What could be so wonderful, and so beloved, that it was named Precious?

It was you.

And just like any proud papa would do, the little light smiled and declared to all of creation, "In a place where once there was nothing, now there is everything."

YOUR PLACE IN THE UNIVERSE

"You are a miracle of creation."

Once upon a time the universe was very different that it is now.

In fact, NASA tells us that at one time, about fourteen billion years ago; the universe was collected together in just one point in space. Of course, as everyone knows, it is not that way anymore.

Edwin Hubble discovered that our universe is rapidly expanding.

In fact, it is now widely believed that there are at least one hundred billion galaxies in the universe. NASA scientists have estimated that our own Milky Way has between 100 billion to 1 trillion stars. Amazingly, each of these stars could have its own planetary system.

These awesome estimations are enough to blow your mind. They are mind boggling to say the least.

However, although these numbers are highly staggering, they are nothing in size and scope compared to everything else within our universe.

So what is this "everything else"? Well, most everything else in the universe is black holes. That's right. Surprisingly, about 95% of our universe is composed of a combination of dark energy and dark matter known as black holes.

Contrary to what one may assume, black holes are not empty spaces in the universe. This is due to the fact that they really are not empty at all. Black holes consist of matter and energy. In fact, there is so much matter crammed into a black hole, nothing can escape … not even light. All these facts about the universe are indeed mind boggling. Amazing. Even thrilling. The scientific estimations of scale for the stars, galaxies, planetary systems, and black holes are really hard to wrap your mind around. All of these huge numbers are just too difficult to even imagine.

Where is your place in all this grand cosmic awesomeness?

Think about it this way. You are either an outlier or you are the whole reason why the universe was created.

After all, since 95% of our universe is composed of black holes, a mega zillion stars, and at least one hundred billion galaxies, the very fact that you exist in this vast universe is a miracle.

Stay in Touch!

If you enjoyed this book, I would be honored if you would please leave a review on Amazon.com.

Sign up for Nancy's inspirational newsletters at: www.nancymarlowe.com/letyoursoulshine

Contact Nancy at: nancy@nancymarlowe.com or www.nancymarlowe.com.

Made in United States
Orlando, FL
14 September 2022

22404842R00093